WILLIAMS BURG

A PICTURE MEMORY

Text
Bill Harris

Captions
Fleur Robertson

Design
Teddy Hartshorn

Photography
Colour Library Books Ltd

Commissioning Editor
Andrew Preston

Editorial
Fleur Robertson

Production
Ruth Arthur
Sally Connolly
David Proffit
Andrew Whitelaw
Karen Staff

Director of Production
Gerald Hughes

CLB 2860
© 1992 Colour Library Books Ltd, Godalming, Surrey, England.
All rights reserved.
This 1992 edition published by Crescent Books,
distributed by Outlet Book Company, Inc., a Random House Company,
40 Engelhard Avenue, Avenel, New Jersey, 07001.
Printed and bound in Singapore.
ISBN 0 517 07274 2
8 7 6 5 4 3 2 1

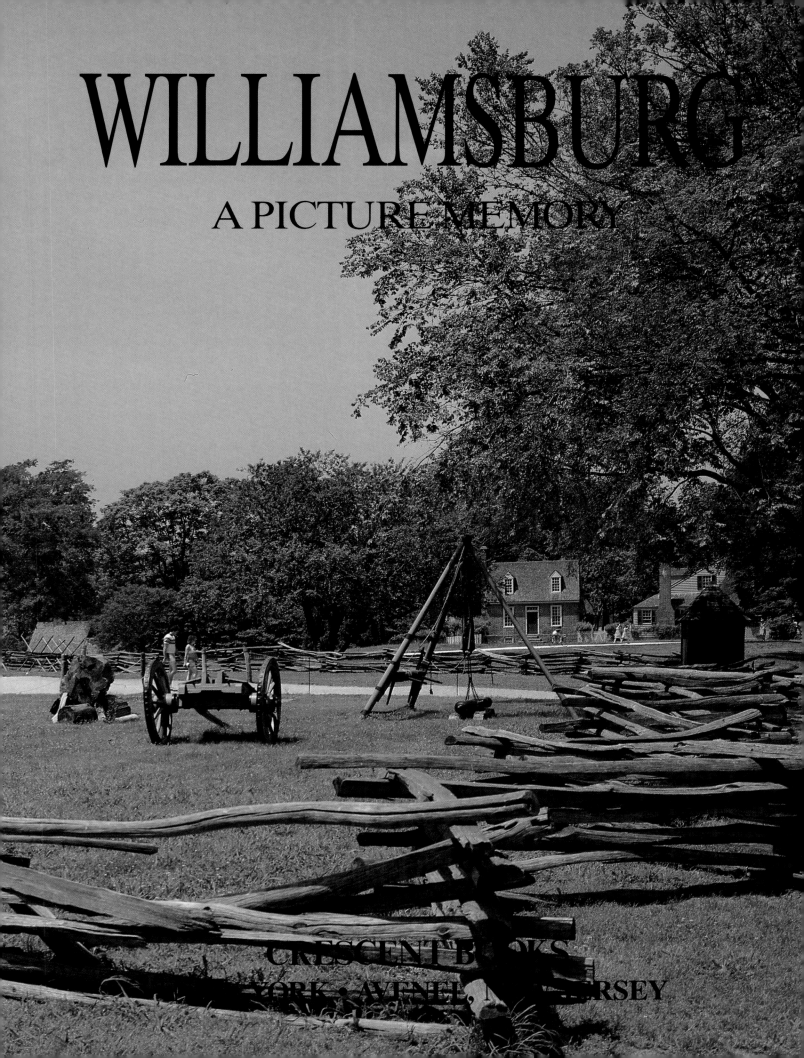

WILLIAMSBURG

A PICTURE MEMORY

CRESCENT BOOKS
NEW YORK · AVENEL, NEW JERSEY

Never ask an American where he is from. If he is from Virginia, he'll tell you without being asked. If he is not, why humiliate him?

Almost no one who was born in Virginia hasn't heard words to that effect. No one who has ever been to Virginia fails to understand them. There is pride in every corner of the Old Dominion. But the corner where it is felt most strongly is between Norfolk and Fredericksburg, and it reaches its highest intensity in the peninsula formed by the York and James rivers. That is where America began. Why shouldn't they be proud?

There are dozens of historic sites in that triangle. The remnants of the first permanent English settlement in North America can still be seen at Jamestown. The battlefield where America finally won its independence from the Mother Country is nearby at Yorktown. The area is dotted with other battlefields important in the Civil War. The capital of the Confederacy is not far away at Richmond.

But in the center of it all is the historic monument more Americans recognize than any other, the second capital of the first colony, Williamsburg.

The amazing thing about Williamsburg is that no one thought of it sooner. Jamestown served as the colonial capital for nearly 100 years, and though it's a pretty place today, it was pretty awful back in the seventeenth century. It wasn't that it was a site casually selected. Three ships with about 140 immigrants aboard were blown into Chesapeake Bay by a storm on April 26, 1607. It took them until May 12 to find a likely place to land and establish their colony. They picked a peninsula on the James River because it was easy to defend against the Indians, who seemed hostile, and because deep water ran close enough to the shore to allow them to tie their boats to the trees on the shoreline. They probably should have moved on. The water wasn't fit to drink. The humidity was worse than oppressive. They had

brought a few chickens along with them, but even they couldn't survive the living conditions. Mosquitoes could, though, and so could weevils who, in fact, thrived on the settlers' store of wheat. By the end of the summer, fifty of the original settlers were dead and the survivors were in the mood for killing each other.

Fortunately, they had some resourceful leaders, like Captain John Smith, and the Indians didn't prove to be as hostile as they had seemed at first. New colonists arrived and there was talk of moving further inland. But with new colonists came new reasons for conflict among them, and by the end of 1609 they had squabbled themselves into almost complete starvation. They managed to turn the Indians against them and by the following spring made a decision to abandon the colony and go home to England. By that point there were only sixty survivors.

They actually did leave on June 10, but before they were clear of the Bay, they met a little fleet of ships sent out from London with a new governor aboard, not to mention new settlers and new supplies.

The new governor, Lord Delaware, had strong ideas about law and order and by the end of the summer he had rebuilt Jamestown and given it a sense of style that affects some Virginians even today. The colony grew after that, and began to spread outward. Life wasn't without its problems. They had them with Indians and with each other. But they thrived in spite of their problems, and many families even grew wealthy. Within less than a dozen years they had their own representative form of government. It was called the General Assembly of Virginia. One of its two parts was a group of Councilors appointed by the London Company — the merchants in England who financed the settlement. The other, called the Burgesses, was composed of men elected by the freemen of the colony itself. The Governor, a royal appointee, had complete veto power, and no laws passed by the Assembly were considered valid without the approval of the London Company.

The Company was more interested in profits than a well-run colony. In the years between 1610 and 1622, 14,000 people went to Jamestown to find a new life. All but 1,000 of them found death. It was one of the great disasters in the history of mankind. No plague, no war has ever taken such a large proportion of a population in so short a time. The most terrible chapter in that story came in 1622 when the Indians went on the warpath and in a single night killed 350 men, women and children.

When the survivors asked the London Company for help, the response was to "send money, go to church, and quit complaining." The king finally responded by forcing the Company's investors to save the colony from starvation. They didn't move quickly enough to suit him and so he revoked their charter and took charge himself.

King James died a few months after that, to the relief of the Burgesses who knew of his opinion of representative government. His son, Charles I, was not much more enlightened about such things, but problems at home kept him distracted. In an almost absent-minded gesture, he told them that they could hold two annual elections. They did. Then they held a third and, when the king's wrath didn't come down on them, a fourth. After their tenth election, Charles took notice of them again. He decreed that no laws or taxes could be imposed without the approval of the General Assembly and reaffirmed that his appointed governor would, in turn, appoint the members of the Council. A point that eluded him was that the governor's appointees were by then all colonists. Unwittingly, Charles I established self-government in England's North American colonies.

Charles didn't seem to give a lot of thought to his selection of governors, but the colony survived. But not long before the king was tossed into prison by Oliver Cromwell, he made a fateful choice in the person of Sir William Berkeley. The governor was replaced twice during the Cromwell Protectorate, both times by men the Virginians violently disliked. The colonists were still loyal to the imprisoned king and when he was beheaded, the Assembly declared that his son, Charles II, was the new king, even though no such declaration was made back in London, and wouldn't be for nearly a dozen years.

During the years of the Protectorate, families still loyal to the monarchy were encouraged to find refuge in Virginia and a huge number answered the call. They all found a warm welcome from fellow Cavaliers, especially former governor Berkeley. When the monarchy was restored and Charles II was officially made king, Berkeley was reinstated as governor and the king had as loyal a group of subjects in Virginia as anywhere in his realm.

The Cavaliers were completely in charge. Anyone Berkeley liked could have the best plantations, the best-paying jobs in public service, even seats in the House of Burgesses. Under Berkeley's tenure, no elections were held for fifteen years.

It led to the first American Revolution. It all began exactly one hundred years before the second one.

It started with new Indian troubles. When the Senecas and Susquehannas began attacking outlying plantations, the governor turned a deaf ear to pleas for help. Forts that had been established were useless because money that had been appropriated to keep them in repair had found its way into Cavalier pockets instead.

The man who brought the planters together against the governor was a Cavalier himself, a former council member named Nathaniel Bacon. He formed his own militia and took care of the Indian problem, then he turned his attention to Jamestown. The governor had suspended him from the Council and branded him a traitor for taking the law into his own hands. Sensing that he had the support of most of the people, Bacon led a 250-man army into Jamestown demanding to see the governor. Berkeley finally agreed to pardon him, and gave him permission to keep on fighting Indians. But Bacon had no sooner left town with his men than the governor revoked the pardon and began saying nasty things about him again. Bacon was accurate in his perception that he had the support of the man in the street and by the time he got back to Jamestown with fire in his eye, he found the governor's mansion empty. Berkeley had fled to the Eastern Shore and Bacon seemed to have been left in charge.

When the Indian fighter left again, after having formed his own government, the governor came home with a small army. Bacon was able to drive him out again, and, as the governor's ships were sailing down the river, he burned Jamestown to the ground.

In a matter of weeks Bacon was dead of malaria, a common affliction in the mosquito-ridden Tidewater country. Berkeley was in charge again and began rounding up the rebels and hanging them. He hanged so many without the formality of a trial that the king ordered him home and appointed a replacement.

Before the former governor died, Charles said of Berkeley:

"The old fool hath put to death more people in that naked country than I did here for the murder of my father."

Bacon had left Virginia with an odd problem. He had burned down its capital. His followers had retreated a few miles up the river to a place called Middle Plantation, a community of a few houses and the church of Bruton Parish which had been established in 1674. They joined with others in a movement to build a new capital there and it seemed to be an idea whose time had come. It was on high ground where there were fewer mosquitoes and the summers were cooler. It was a more central location that was easily reached by boat from inland plantations.

But instead, the men in charge rebuilt the Jamestown State House and its church and for the next several years swatted bugs and fended off riots over the price of tobacco from the same old stand.

In 1689, the same year William and Mary became the joint sovereigns of England, Dr. James Blair was appointed Commissary of the Church in Virginia. Of all the parishes he visited, his overwhelming favorite was Bruton Parish, which he selected to be the site of a college everyone agreed the colony needed.

The colony itself cooperated by levying a tax on tobacco to pay for the college, and he went off to England where he received a charter from William and Mary, as well as badly-needed funds. He also received a royal appointment to head the institution, a position he held for the next fifty years.

It wasn't easy establishing the college, but Dr. Blair was a tenacious man. It sputtered to life at Middle Plantation in 1695 with a staff of three: the president, a writing master and an "usher." The College of William and Mary was soon housed in a magnificent building designed by no less a person than Sir Christopher Wren, who said that his plan had been "adapted to the nature of the country by the gentlemen there." In spite of the apparent tampering by a committee, the building turned out to be the most magnificent in the entire British Empire. In the years since, it has survived "improvements" by later architects as well as two major fires. Today it has been restored to its original appearance

and it is still one of the great buildings in the entire world, not to mention its status as the only building in America by the great architect of Saint Paul's Cathedral in London.

Not long after construction began, the State House in Jamestown was destroyed by fire and the idea of moving it to another city was raised again. Since Middle Plantation had such a beautiful place for the Assembly to meet, the governor decided to move it there. In the legislation that made it possible, it was also decided to rename the town Williamsburg in honor of the king. Privately-owned buildings on the 300-acre site were bought and torn down to make way for a planned city that would be the envy of America and even the world.

The governor, Francis Nicholson, ordered that every building lot must be no less than a half-acre to allow room for a house, a garden and an orchard. He specified the distance from the street to the front door of every house should be at least six feet. Every lot was required to be fenced or walled within six months after the house was built. In these days of suburban zoning regulations, these rules don't seem at all unusual. But in 1699 they must have raised a lot of eyebrows in freedom-loving Virginia.

The governor specified that the city should have a broad main street a mile long between the college and the capitol. It would be ninety feet wide and named Duke of Gloucester Street. Halfway along its length would be a market square and at right angles to it would be another broad avenue leading to the governor's home, which would be called a "palace."

He had a great sense of politics, and proposed that the city should take the form of a monogram of the letters "W" and "M" to honor the king and queen. No one dared tell him that such an arrangement would have streets dropping off into ravines. Fortunately, he figured that out for himself and proposed an alternative based on a plan advanced thirty years before by Sir Christopher Wren for rebuilding the City of London after the Great Fire.

Lacking a monogram, he named the streets after the children of the monarchs. The Duke of Gloucester was the son of the queen. Another street was named for Prince George, husband of Princess Anne and Nassau Street was named for the ancestral family of the king.

Governor Nicholson was something of a tyrant, and

was finally recalled. He was replaced by a man with the ironic name of Nott, who did little more for Williamsburg than leaving his name on a tombstone in Bruton churchyard. The real work of building Williamsburg and making it an important city fell on the shoulders of Alexander Spotswood, who became governor in 1710.

The job took more than ten years, during which time the streets were paved, the Governor's Palace built and Nicholson's personal coat of arms removed from the Capitol building.

Though it was among the most important cities in Colonial America, the population of Williamsburg, slaves and all, never went higher than about 2000. When the Assembly wasn't in session, it was a sleepy little country town. But when the government came to life, so did the city. The plays of William Shakespeare were presented in the evenings, featuring actors imported from London. People dressed in the height of London fashion, too. The entertaining by important people who had townhouses there was done on a lavish scale. The taverns were open all night and residents were kept awake by almost nightly fireworks displays.

But for all its importance to the history of America, Williamsburg's heyday lasted less than sixty years. When Thomas Jefferson was elected governor in 1779, British troops had already passed through Williamsburg and were threatening to come back. Jefferson proposed that the capital be moved to Richmond and when his advice was taken a year later, Williamsburg became a sleepy little college town again.

Even its history was largely forgotten by 1903 when the Rev. Dr. W.A.R. Goodwin accepted the call to become rector of Bruton Parish Church. A town native, he was dismayed by the decay that had set in even in his lifetime. He was passionate about changing it for the better and within four years he had raised enough money to restore his church to its original splendor in time for the 300th anniversary of the Episcopal Church in America. But nobody thought the whole town would ever be restored.

Dr. Goodwin moved on to Rochester, New York in 1909 and returned in 1923 to join the faculty of William and Mary. He came back with his enthusiasm intact and fortunately was able to pass some of it along to the philanthropist John D. Rockefeller, Jr. Almost no one in town didn't agree that the combination of Dr. Goodwin's passion and Mr. Rockefeller's money was the best thing that happened to Williamsburg since Governor Nicholson gave up the idea of having its streets laid out in the form of a William and Mary monogram.

On February 24, 1934, less than six years and $12 million after the restoration began, the Virginia Assembly crowded itself into the Capitol at Williamsburg for the first time in more than 150 years and officially welcomed the past back to Virginia.

The building isn't the original, but it would fool any of the original settlers. The old capitol, like so many of the Williamsburg buildings, had long since disappeared. But they have been rebuilt using original plans and, whenever possible materials from the same sources.

The Williamsburg restoration is one of the most ambitious architectural projects of the twentieth century. Millions have walked its streets and taken away ideas that have changed the face of other towns all over America. It created a national interest in "recycling" rather than destroying old buildings. And all the current interest in "early American" architecture and decoration can be traced to this recreation of Colonial Williamsburg. The Keeper of the National Register of Historic Places has said that Williamsburg is the "formulator of popular twentieth century taste" in America.

What could be more appropriate? In its relatively short life as Virginia's capital, Williamsburg was almost the formulator of America itself.

Facing page: the Capitol, a perfect replica of the original.

Part of the Governor's Palace (right) and all of Bruton Parish Church (facing page) was designed by Alexander Spotswood, governor of Williamsburg. Bruton was completed in 1769 after the addition of its tower. One of America's oldest churches, it has been in continuous use since 1775. It was the Reverend W. A. R. Goodwin, the Episcopal rector of Bruton, who, in 1926, was to convince the millionaire, John D. Rockefeller, Jr., to restore Williamsburg to its former colonial glory. At that time, all that was proposed was the restoration of small areas around the church, the Market Square and the Capitol. The project grew as Mr. Rockefeller became more interested in the town's potential. Below: the Courthouse of 1770, where on July 26, 1776, the Declaration of Independence was proclaimed from the steps to the people of Williamsburg, with accompanying illuminations and the firing of cannons and muskets. The building served Williamsburg and James City County in its capacity as a working court until 1932. Today it has been restored, refurnished and reopened as a colonial county courthouse, the focus of local government in the eighteenth century. Most cases that came before the bench here two hundred years ago concerned violations of apprenticeships, disputes over land, and suits for payments of debt. Crimes such as murder, arson and robbery – all of which were hanging offences – were tried in the General Court that convened twice annually in the Capitol. As the center of a busy life and the site of the regular Wednesday and Saturday town markets, the Market Square on which the Courthouse stands would also have been the site of the much larger, twice-yearly town fair, when livestock was sold and a variety of entertainments, such as puppet shows, beauty contests, cockfights, dancing and fiddling for prizes, were to be enjoyed.

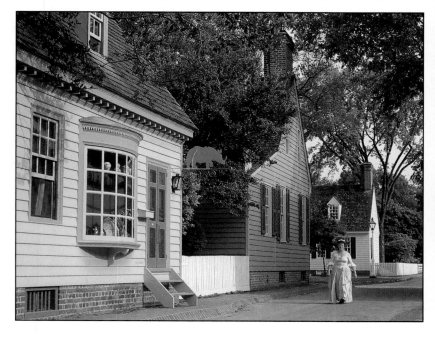

Left: costumed staff enjoy the sun outside the Raleigh Tavern. Below left: a matched pair of horses pull a carriage down Duke of Gloucester Street. Along this most important of Williamsburg's thoroughfares can be found The Sign of the Rhinoceros (bottom left), the reconstructed and privately occupied apothecary, as well as the Printing Office (below), which stands on the site of the eighteenth-century original. Overleaf: the Margaret Hunter Shop, a milliner's, and The Golden Ball, a colonial jewelry shop.

Facing page top: a typical Williamsburg house with a stepped redbrick chimney identical to those seen on houses in Tudor England. Despite its earlier chimney design, the sash windows identify this as a Georgian building. Facing page bottom: Prentis Store of 1740, one of Williamsburg's best examples of shop architecture, and (below) Nicholson's Shop, which has been restored around its original frame, on Duke of Gloucester Street.

Below: Peyton Randolph House, whose owner was one of the leading statesmen of colonial America. Randolph, a cousin of Thomas Jefferson, was elected president of the First Continental Congress in 1774. Right: John Greenhow House and Store, and (below right) Archibald Blair House, one of the most elegant frame houses in Williamsburg, which was acquired by Dr. Blair in 1716. Bottom right: James Anderson House, the former home of Anderson, a blacksmith and Virginia's public armorer.

These pages: the civic buildings of Colonial Williamsburg. Left: the somber Public Gaol, which served as the city jail of Williamsburg until 1910. Its most infamous inmates were Blackbeard's pirates, thirteen of whom were hanged after their trial in the General Court. Below left: the Courthouse of 1770, and (bottom left) the Governor's Palace and its formal and elaborate eighteenth-century gardens. Below: the Guardhouse and Magazine that held the colony's military equipment.

The most important public building in Colonial Williamsburg was the Capitol (these pages). It was here that the House of Burgesses, America's oldest representative assembly, met in the plainly decorated Hall of Burgesses (left). The Capitol was also where the Governor's Council met, though their room (below and facing page top) upstairs was considerably more ornate. The Council comprised twelve wealthy and prominent men chosen by the British king to advise the governor. Council members also served as judges in the highest court in the colony, the General Court (facing page bottom), which met in the Capitol. As time wore on, the Burgesses started to voice the objections of the people they represented against the restrictive practices imposed on the colonists by the British government. Naturally, the Governor's Council supported the king's position. In 1769, when the House of Burgesses opposed an act that inflicted yet another tax on the colony, the governor dissolved the House, but this action – designed to take the heat out of the situation – failed to intimidate the representatives. Within seven years, they were so opposed to British rule, and the governor who represented it, that they voted unanimously to adopt the Virginia Resolutions for Independence, thus severing their ties with the Motherland for good. A month later the last British Governor of Virginia, Lord Dunmore, was on a ship sailing for home. The Capitol fell into disuse after the Revolution when Virginia's government was transferred to Richmond. The H-shaped Capitol building (overleaf) on show in Williamsburg today is a reconstruction, built on the original foundations, which was opened in 1934.

Facing page: (top) one of Williamsburg's smaller residences, and
(bottom) the Pitt-Dixon House. Dr. George Pitt opened an apothecary
shop here, The Sign of the Rhinoceros, later selling the property to the
printer John Dixon in 1774, when the house was over fifty years old.
Below: the apparently stone-faced Pasteur-Galt Apothecary Shop.
Wooden boarding could be made to look like stone by a process known
as rustication – shaping the wood to resemble stone blocks.

Facing page top: the ceremonial "Volley of Joy" fired by the Colonial Williamsburg Militia on Market Square after readings from the Declaration of Independence – part of Williamsburg's Fourth of July celebrations. A cannon salute (facing page bottom) follows and cheers are given by the militia's musketeers (below). The tribute concludes with the ringing of Virginia's "Liberty Bell" in Bruton Church tower, just as it rang in 1776 when the Declaration of Independence was adopted.

31

Over a hundred of the costumed inhabitants of Colonial Williamsburg serve as master craftsmen, journeymen and apprentices in a variety of craft shops, such as a boot maker's (facing page top), a baker's (facing page bottom), a candle maker's (right), and a cabinet maker's (below). The craftsmen work with the types of tools used by their predecessors in colonial days, making the articles that were common then, such as barrels in the cooper's shop (above). Many such wares are for sale. In summer, outdoor craft demonstrations are given for visitors, during which craftsmen answer questions in eighteenth-century fashion.

34

These pages: authentically costumed staff at Colonial Williamsburg bring the eighteenth century to life. Actors dressed as servants, artisans, prosperous merchants, soldiers and slaves unselfconsciously go about their business, curtsying and bowing to their "betters" when appropriate, and happily explaining to the public their tasks and routines. There are no set lectures, just the sharing of the good-natured gossip concerning topics that would have been current then.

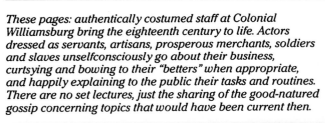

Below: the Davidson Shop, once the apothecary shop of Robert Davidson, a "Practitioner in Physick" and mayor of Williamsburg in 1738. The shop later helped to support the widow Sarah Waters, who rented it out. Facing page top: John Blair House, former home of one of the first Supreme Court judges, John Blair Jr., appointed by Washington. The Blairs, who originally came from Scotland, were one of Williamsburg's first families. Facing page bottom: the Orlando Jones House and Office. "Office" was the name of any small building that lacked a specific use.

39

Visitors (left) to Colonial Williamsburg find they are walking into the past, where no cars are allowed and only regular musket-firing disturbs the quiet in the streets. Below left and bottom left: the John Blair House, the easterly part of which was built in the early eighteenth century. This restoration is of one of the oldest houses in Williamsburg. Below: the handsome George Wythe House, home of one of the most distinguished Americans of his time, and (overleaf) sun on the Orlando Jones House.

Facing page top: the Greenhow-Repiton House and the neighboring Boot and Shoemaker's Shop. An eighteenth-century shoemaker could make, on average, two pairs of shoes a day. He usually worked with a straight last, as in those times shoes that made no distinction between right and left were thought elegant. Facing page bottom: the tree-shaded silversmith's shop that belonged to James Geddy, and (below) the Margaret Hunter Shop, an original building that houses a milliner's wares.

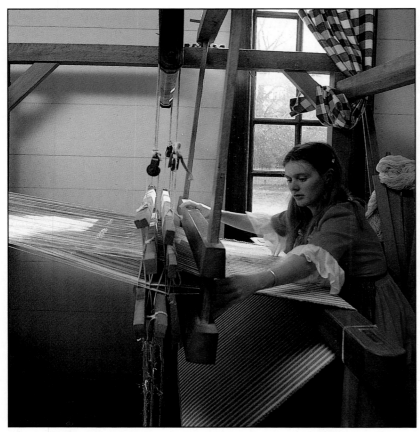

Left: weaving in Colonial Williamsburg, just one of a variety of skills that provided the everyday requirements of this eighteenth-century town. Wool spinning in preparation for weaving was undertaken by women, while basket making (facing page top) was a household task often undertaken by slaves. Some crafts, however, required extensive training, and these often formed the basis of thriving businesses. Examples of such would be jewelry-making (above), millinery (facing page bottom) and the inventing of remedies such as those to be found today in Pasteur-Galt's Apothecary's Shop (below). Overleaf: a carriage rolls slowly through Market Square.

47

The original Raleigh Tavern burned in 1859 and its reconstruction (these pages) was built with reference to engravings of the time. The tavern was the center of Williamsburg's business and political activities and the forum for such colonial leaders as Thomas Jefferson, Patrick Henry and George Washington. The House of Burgesses even convened in the tavern's Apollo Room on the two occasions when the governor dissolved the assembly – the Raleigh became, in effect, the unofficial capitol.

Colonial Williamsburg's taverns numbered more than ten during the town's heyday. They ranged from the large and inexpensive, such as Christiana Campbell's Tavern (below) and Chowning's Tavern (overleaf), to the more elegant, such as the Raleigh (below right) and Wetherburn's (bottom right), which could offer private rooms, such as the Raleigh's Daphne Room and Wetherburn's Bull's Head Room, for parties and business meetings. Right: part of Merchants Square.

This page: snow notwithstanding, the State Garrison and Williamsburg's Fife and Drum Corps parade on Market Square and on the Palace Green as part of the Christmas holiday celebrations in Colonial Williamsburg. The State Garrison's collection of arms, military equipment and ammunition (facing page) is displayed in the Magazine. It includes a number of flintlock muskets – the standard arm of all British and colonial troops in the eighteenth century.

Carter's Grove (these pages), an eighteenth-century mansion, lies on the James River six miles from Williamsburg. Completed by the plantation owner Carter Burwell in 1755, the house was owned by five generations of his family. Today the property is cared for by the Colonial Williamsburg Foundation. Known particularly for its superbly crafted interior woodwork (above and below), the mansion bears the scars of a British visit during the Revolution, when Colonel Tarleton is said to have ridden his horse up the staircase (facing page bottom), slashing the rail with his saber as he went. The deep cuts remain to this day. Carter's Grove also boasts the famous "Refusal Room," the parlor where both Jefferson and Washington had their proposals of marriage rejected by early loves. It is said their chosen ladies waited to marry gentlemen with more promising careers.

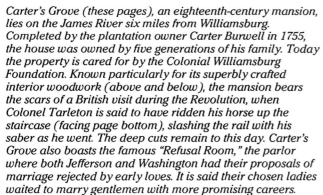

Facing page top: early morning light along Duke of
Gloucester Street, where the King's Arms Tavern (below) has
welcomed patrons for many years. In its day, this was held as
one of the most "genteel" taverns in Colonial Williamsburg.
Facing page bottom: the town's walled Magazine, and
(overleaf) Market Square Tavern. Following page:
Robertson's Windmill, the town's reconstructed working mill.

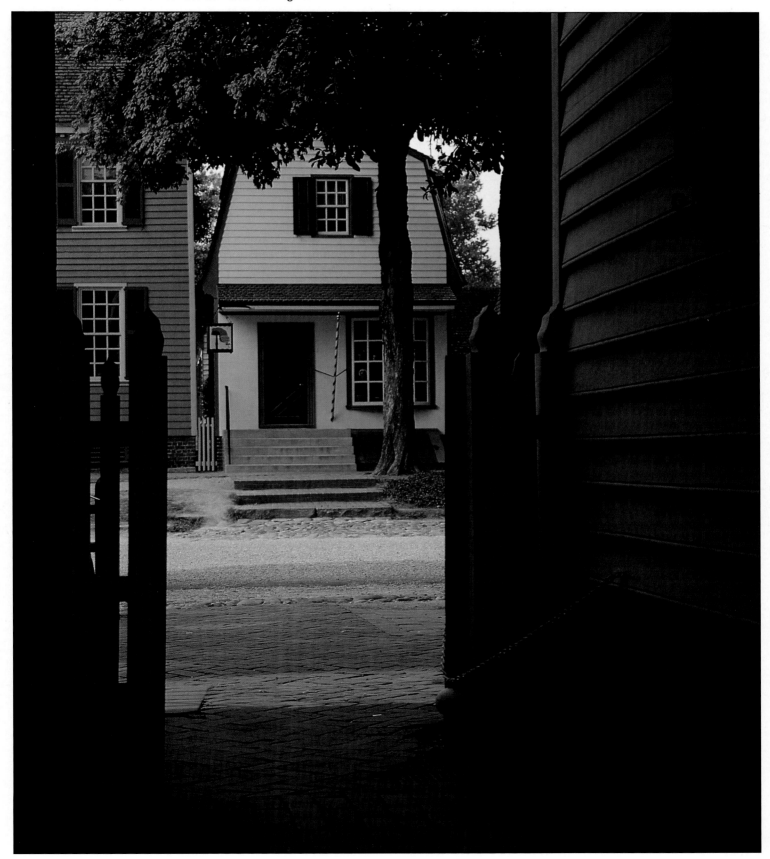